23.99

capstone
3/19

dabblelab

EPIC
CARDBOARD
ADVENTURES

EXPLORE THE WORLD
→ with ←

CARDBOARD
(& DUCT TAPE)

BY

LESLIE MANLAPIG

4D™

AN AUGMENTED READING
CARDBOARD
EXPERIENCE

CAPSTONE PRESS
a capstone imprint

TABLE OF CONTENTS

Download the Capstone 4D app!

STEP 1 Ask an adult to search in the Apple App Store or Google Play for "Capstone 4D".

STEP 2 Click Install (Android) or Get, then Install (Apple).

STEP 3 Open the app.

STEP 4 Scan any of the following spreads with this icon:

Watch some fun videos!

When you scan a spread, you'll find fun extra stuff to go with this book! You can also find these things on the web at www.capstone4D.com using the password: cardboard.explore

YOUR ADVENTURE STARTS
↓ HERE ↓↓

Have you dreamed of exploring the world? This book will help you do that and more, using . . .

CARDBOARD!

≥ Yes, that's right! ≤

The boxes sitting around your house can be used to make your very own adventures. All you need are some simple supplies and a willing adult to help you with sharp tools.

Don't forget to check out the 4D videos to help guide you through the steps. Also, we've included many templates to help you complete projects in this book. Just scan this star!

Before you know it, you'll be sitting in your very own spaceship wearing snowshoes!

SUPPLIES

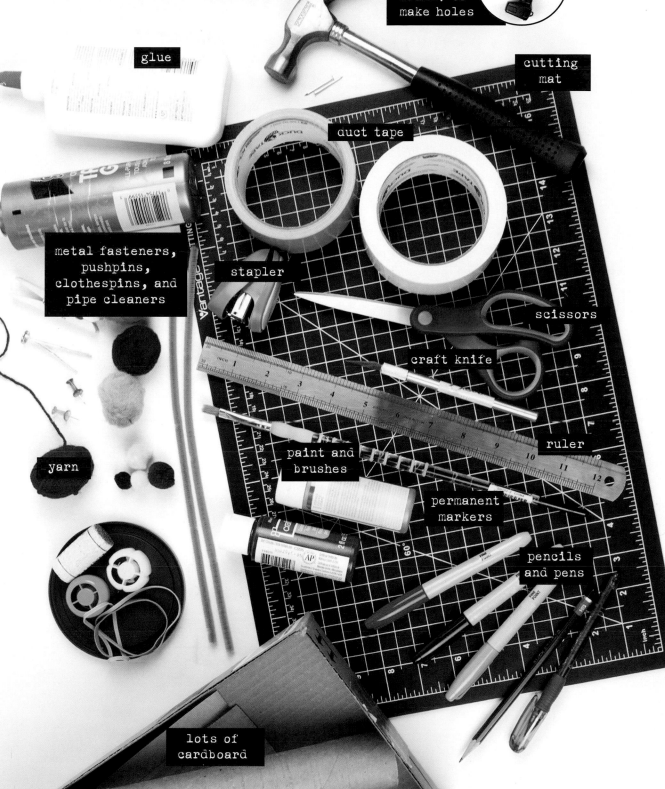

hammer and nails (or a drill) to make holes

glue

cutting mat

duct tape

metal fasteners, pushpins, clothespins, and pipe cleaners

stapler

scissors

craft knife

yarn

paint and brushes

ruler

permanent markers

pencils and pens

lots of cardboard

PROJECT #1

SPACE SHUTTLE

Ever wonder how a space shuttle blasts off into space? Powerful rocket boosters and an external fuel tank thrust the space shuttle into orbit. Once they are no longer needed. The rocket boosters and fuel tank detach from the shuttle. Recreate this amazing launch sequence with this easy-to-build cardboard toy!

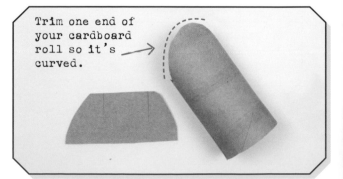

SUPPLIES

- scissors
- 1 paper towel roll
- cardboard (use thin, non-corrugated cereal box cardboard)
- 1 toilet paper roll
- white and red paint
- paintbrush
- black and orange permanent markers
- orange and white duct tape
- hot glue gun
- hook and loop fastener (optional)

1 Cut your paper towel roll into two unequal rolls.

The longer roll will be your fuel tank.

The shorter roll will be your space shuttle.

2 (For space shuttle)

Cut out a tail piece from the cereal box. Cut one slit on each side so it attaches to your cardboard roll. Cut out matching slits into your paper towel roll.

Trim one end of your cardboard roll so it's curved.

3 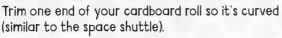 **(For external fuel tank)**
Trim one end of your cardboard roll so it's curved (similar to the space shuttle).

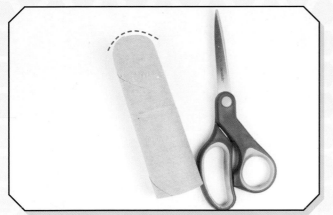

4 **(For rocket boosters)**
Cut your toilet roll tube in half lengthwise. Trim one end of each so they're curved.

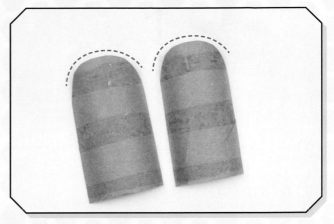

5 Paint your space shuttle (white), external fuel tank (red), and rocket boosters (white). Use permanent markers or duct tape to add extra detail. Roll up your rockets and use duct tape to secure them.

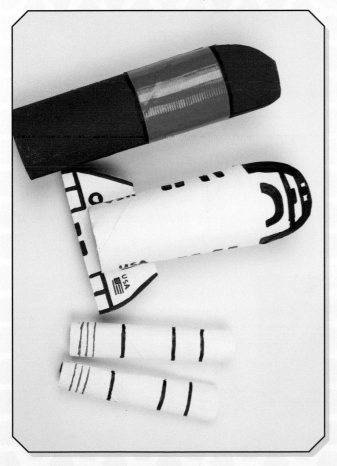

6 Hot glue your rockets, space shuttle, and fuel tank together.

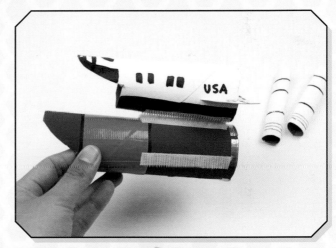

TIP

1. You can use white glue instead of a hot glue gun, though it will take longer to dry.

2. Use the hook and loop fastener to give this project a more realistic touch!

PROJECT #2

SPACESHIP CONTROLS

It's 20 years in the future. You're an astronaut ready to take your first flight. Where would you fly? What would the inside of your spaceship look like? It's time to build your dream ride!

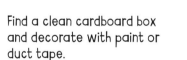

SUPPLIES

- cardboard box
- duct tape
- various everyday items: bottle caps, egg cartons, calculators, stickers, black paper, clothespins, magnets, metal lids, golf tees, CDs, plastic lids, buttons, old electronic equipment, plastic bottles, rubber bands, skewers
- cutting mat
- scissors
- black paper
- white pencil
- glue (hot glue or tacky glue)
- drill (or hammer and nail)

1 Find a clean cardboard box and decorate with paint or duct tape.

2 Look for an assortment of items to use as buttons, dials, screens, and switches.

SEARCH TIP: Look in the recycling bin or use old electronic equipment!

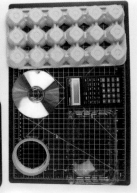

3 (To create screens)

Cut out rectangles and squares from black paper. Use a white pencil to draw on details.

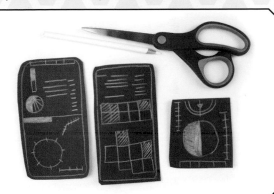

4

Use hot glue, tacky glue, or duct tape to adhere your console.

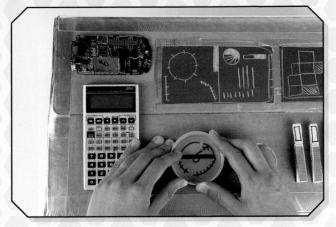

5 (To create a joystick)

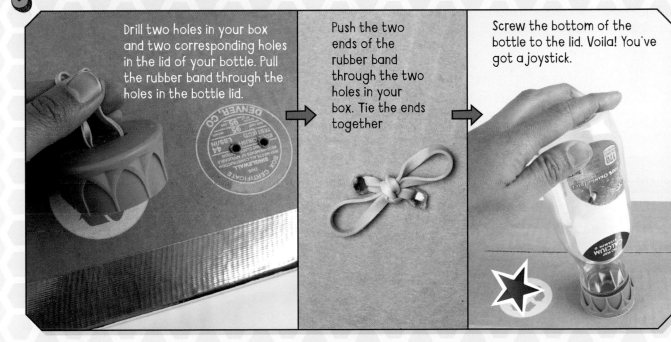

Drill two holes in your box and two corresponding holes in the lid of your bottle. Pull the rubber band through the holes in the bottle lid.

Push the two ends of the rubber band through the two holes in your box. Tie the ends together

Screw the bottom of the bottle to the lid. Voila! You've got a joystick.

TIP

1. Use a skewer to push the rubber band through the holes in the bottle lid.

2. Decorate your console with a permanent marker and duct tape!

3. Ask your adult helper to drill or hammer.

9

PROJECT #3

SPACE HELMET

You've finally blasted into outer space. Congratulations! Are you ready to explore the great beyond? This helmet will help you take one giant leap for humankind!

1 Trim your paper grocery bag so it fits nicely on your head. Paint it black.

2 Sketch and cut out a design for a helmet.

Keep in mind where you want to put your visor.

Tape similarly sized strips of duct tape onto a cutting mat. Make sure they overlap to create a duct tape sheet.

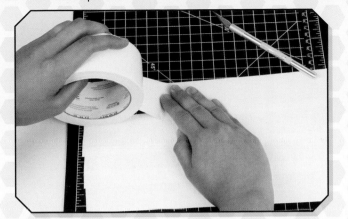

 Place your helmet on top of the duct tape sheet. Trace it and use your craft knife to cut out the helmet.

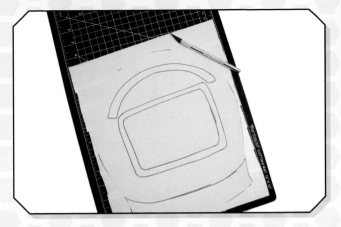

Time to place your visor onto your helmet. Trace a plastic container onto your duct tape helmet. Use your craft knife to cut it out.

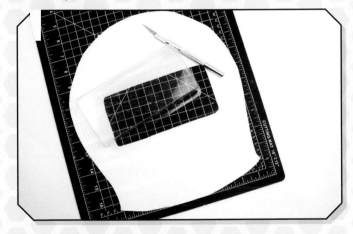

 Stick your duct tape helmet onto your painted paper bag.

Cover corrugated cardboard with duct tape. Hot glue extra elements to the helmet.

Pop in your visor and duct tape it to the helmet on the inside.

Use permanent markers to add extra details to the helmet. Use a white pencil to add stars to space.

PROJECT #1

SCUBA MASK

There are many beautiful and mysterious sea animals. Take a closer look at them with this scuba mask. Happy swimming!

- plastic berry lid
- scissors
- cutting mat
- egg carton

- pencil
- craft knife
- black and green duct tape

- elastic
- stapler

1 Clean your plastic berry lid and let it dry. Cut the lid so it's nice and flat.

2 Cut the lid off of your egg carton. Trace the lid onto the egg carton and cut that portion out with a craft knife. Continue to shape the egg carton into a scuba mask shape. Trim it so it's just a little flatter.

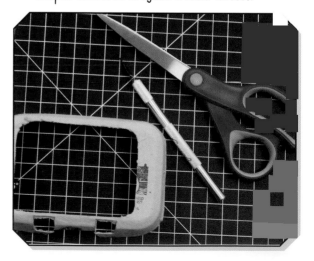

3 Cut out a section on the bottom edge of the egg carton for your nose.

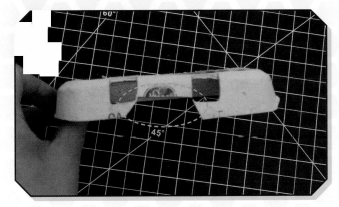

4 Cut out one slit on each side of the egg carton for the strap.

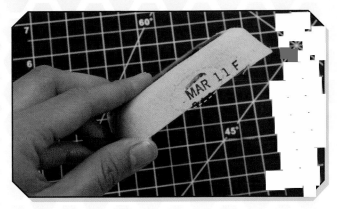

5 Cut strips of duct tape and use them to decorate the egg carton. Additionally, use duct tape to stick your plastic lid on.

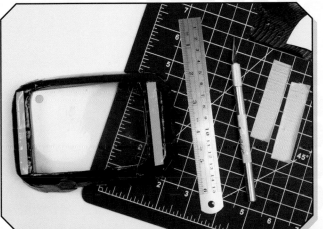

6 To make the strap, slide a strip of elastic through the side slits and staple them together.

Cover up the staples with duct tape.

DON'T HAVE ELASTIC?

TRY THESE INSTEAD!

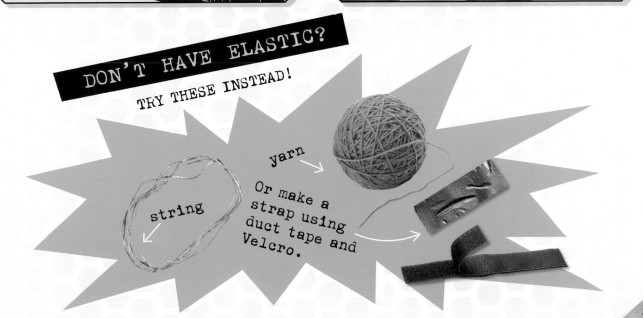

yarn

string

Or make a strap using duct tape and Velcro.

PROJECT #2

BOAT DESIGN

Ready to sail the seven seas? Design and create your very own cardboard boats. You can even test them out on the water!

SUPPLIES

- paper
- pencil
- ruler
- cardboard
- scissors
- craft knife
- cutting mat
- duct tape
- permanent markers
- large container of water (or bathtub or pool)

1 Draw one or more of these designs onto paper to use as templates. Solid lines note where you will cut the cardboard. Dotted lines note where you will score and bend the cardboard.

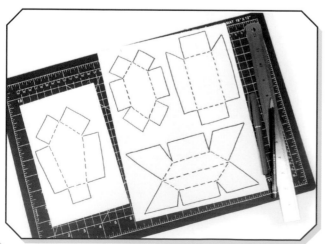

2 Trace the templates directly onto cardboard to make identically sized boats. (Or you can draw larger versions of your templates onto cardboard.) Cut out.

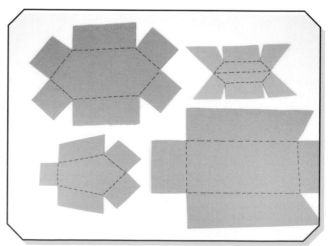

Score the dotted lines with a craft knife (run the knife over the cardboard). Make sure you don't cut completely through the cardboard!

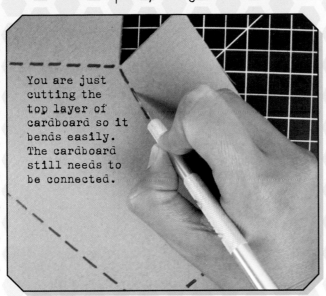

You are just cutting the top layer of cardboard so it bends easily. The cardboard still needs to be connected.

4 Fold up the flaps and tape them together.

5 Decorate your boat with duct tape and permanent markers.

Make sure you use permanent markers. They will not bleed in water.

6 Once you're ready, put your boat in the water. Does it float? Will it carry weight? Which boat design seems to float the best?

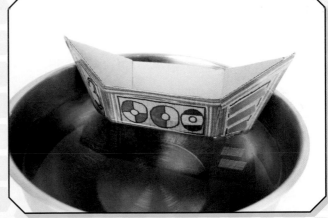

TIP
To make your boat last longer cover it completely with duct tape.

PROJECT #3
SHARK FIN

Ahh! What's that lurking in the water? Scare friends and family by transforming yourself into one of the most frightening ocean predators – a shark!

SUPPLIES

- corrugated cardboard
- scissors
- tacky glue
- paint and paintbrush
- ruler
- duct tape
- craft knife
- cutting mat
- clear tape

1 Cut a rectangle out of cardboard. This will be your back piece. It should sit and fit between your shoulders like a backpack would.

2 Cut out two fin shapes from cardboard. They should be approximately the same length as your back piece

3 Cut out four slits, one in each corner of your back piece. They should be as wide as your duct tape. Also cut out a slit in the middle of your back piece.

TIP
You can also just cut out one fin shape if you're short on time or cardboard.

Cut out a slit in each of the fin pieces. They should be in identical locations.

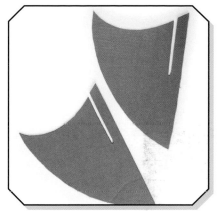

 Use tacky glue to glue your fin pieces together.

Paint your fin and back piece.

7 (To make duct tape straps)

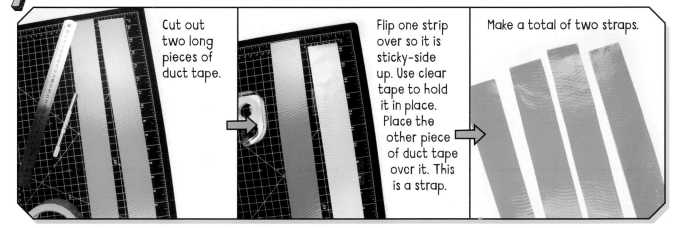

Cut out two long pieces of duct tape.

Flip one strip over so it is sticky-side up. Use clear tape to hold it in place. Place the other piece of duct tape over it. This is a strap.

Make a total of two straps.

8 Slide the fin into the slit in the middle of the back piece. Insert a strap into the slit in one of the corners. Pull it through the slit in the opposite corner, running it the same direction as the fin.

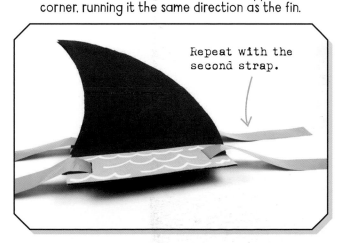

Repeat with the second strap.

9 Use a piece of duct tape to tape the ends of your straps together. Slip the srtaps over your shoulders and you are a shark!

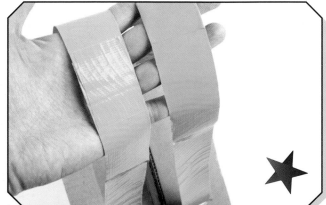

PROJECT #1

ADJUSTABLE BINOCULARS

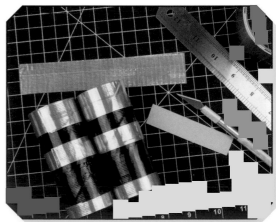

What's that in the distance? Now you'll know! A great explorer needs a great pair of binoculars!

- thin cardboard (non-corrugated)
- scissors
- 2 toilet paper rolls
- gold and black duct tape
- cutting mat
- craft knife
- stapler
- hole punch
- yarn

1 Cut out a small rectangle from thin cardboard.

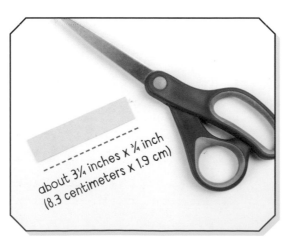

about 3¼ inches x ¾ inch (8.3 centimeters x 1.9 cm)

2 Decorate your toilet paper rolls and thin cardboard rectangle with black and gold duct tape. Trim off any excess tape.

Staple the thin cardboard rectangle between the two toilet paper rolls.

4 Punch a hole on each side of your rolls.

5 Tie a piece of yarn (or string) through the holes in your cardboard rolls.

6 Use duct tape to cover your knots. Now you can use your binoculars to explore!

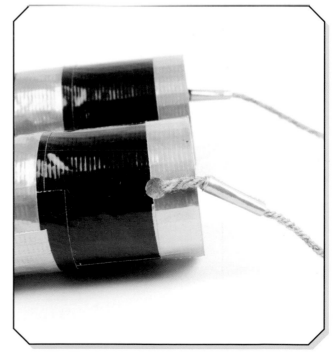

PROJECT #2

CLAWS

What's that shadow moving in the distance? A panther? A lion? Nope. It's you! Experience being the ruler of the jungle with a set of cardboard claws. Rawr!

SUPPLIES

- corrugated cardboard
- scissors
- paint and paintbrush
- pencil
- paper
- hot glue

Cut out six cardboard claws and two cardboard hand bars. The claws should be pointed in front and curved in the back.

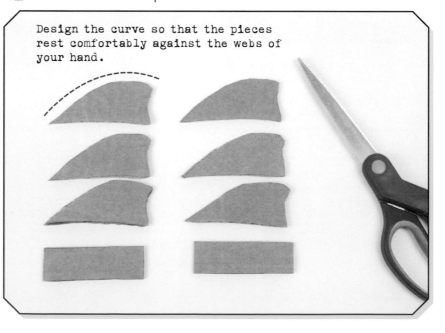

Design the curve so that the pieces rest comfortably against the webs of your hand.

Paint your claws and let them dry.

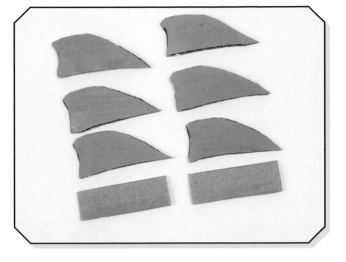

3 Hold a hand bar in your hand so one edge rests in your knuckles. Loosely wrap your fingers around it. Mark the spaces between your fingers. Do this for both hand bars.

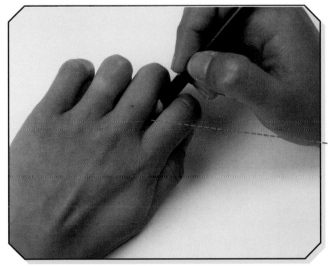

4 Hot glue a claw onto each of the markings.

PROJECT #3

EXPLORER BAG

Ready to go on a great adventure? What will you pack? A compass? Binoculars? First aid kit? Be prepared for any adventure with this duct tape explorer's bag!

SUPPLIES

- paper
- pencil
- scissors
- brown, black, green, orange duct tape
- craft knife
- cutting mat
- trash bag

(To make a template)
Draw one square for the front of the bag and one rectangle for the back. Cut out.

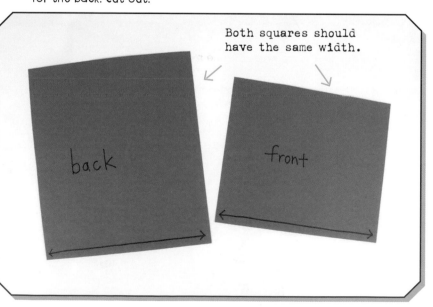

Both squares should have the same width.

back

front

22

(To make the back piece)
Cut out strips of duct tape and stick them together, slightly overlapping each strip. Make sure it's bigger than your template's back rectangle.

 Starting from one corner, carefully peel your sheet of duct tape off the mat. Flip it over so the sticky side is up. Place a sheet of the trash bag onto the sticky side.

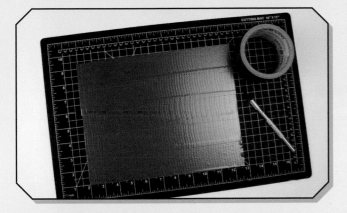

TIP
Rub the garbage bag to get rid of air bubbles and flatten wrinkles.

 Trace your template onto your sheet of duct tape. Cut it out.

 Tape the front and back pieces together. Cut out strips of duct tape to add more design details to your bag.

Repeat steps 2-4 for your front square piece.

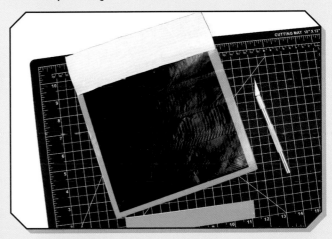

Cut a 16-inch (41-cm) piece of duct tape. Flip it over so the sticky side is up. Fold over one side to the middle, lengthwise. Fold the other side on top of it. Now you have a strap! Tape it to the back of your bag.

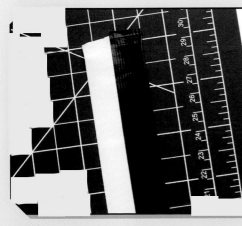

Make more of these straps until you get the correct strap length for your bag.

PROJECT #1

SLED

Every Arctic explorer needs a handy sled to carry materials and friends. Time to sail over the snow with your own creation!

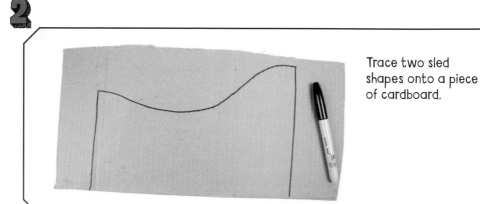

SUPPLIES

- shoe box
- corrugated cardboard
- permanent marker
- scissors
- tacky glue
- paint and paintbrush
- hammer and nail
- yarn

1 Grab a shoe box without the lid.

2 Trace two sled shapes onto a piece of cardboard.

3 Cut out each sled shape.

4 Use tacky glue to attach the two sides of the sled onto the shoe box.

TIP
Place a book on top of the sled to keep the sides in place.

5 Paint the box.

6 Using a hammer and nail, punch two holes in the front of the sled. Then tie a piece of yarn to the sled.

YOU'RE DONE!

With temperatures dropping and night approaching, building your own shelter is essential. But this isn't your normal ice igloo. Yours will be made from cardboard!

PROJECT #2
IGLOO

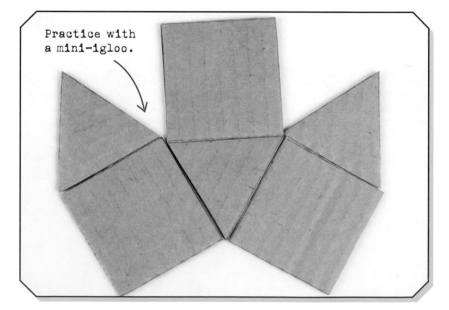

SUPPLIES

- large corrugated cardboard boxes
- scissors
- duct tape
- craft knife (or box cutter)
- cutting mat
- ruler
- tape measure
- paint and paintbrush

 Cut out three equilateral triangles and three squares. An equilateral triangle's sides are all the same length.

Practice with a mini-igloo.

2 Trim duct tape to fit. Tape the pieces together in the arrangement shown below. (steps 2-4 are using a small-scale model)

 3 Attach the two side triangles to the square in between them. Your igloo should now be completely formed.

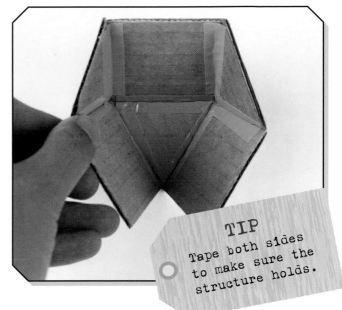

TIP
Tape both sides to make sure the structure holds.

 4 Decorate the igloo with more duct tape or paint.

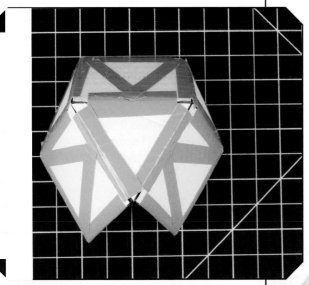

After you've finished using your cardboard igloo, fold it along the seams and pack it away!

HOW LONG SHOULD YOUR PIECES BE?

Well, that depends on your height! Sit down and have someone measure your height seated. You'll need to be able to sit inside your igloo. For an igloo to fit a person who is 26–32 inches (66–81 cm) tall, your pieces must have sides that are between 30–37 inches (76–94 cm) long. Try adding around 5 inches (13 cm) to your seated height, and that should do the trick!

PROJECT #3

SNOWSHOES

Brr! How do arctic explorers travel over snow without sinking? They wear snowshoes! Craft your very own pair of rad snow kicks from cardboard with this fun, wearable craft!

SUPPLIES

- paper for template
- corrugated cardboard
- shoe
- pencil
- scissors
- craft knife
- cutting mat
- tacky glue
- duct tape (orange, silver, yellow)
- clear tape

1 Trace around your shoe to make a template for your snowshoes. Cut out your template.

2 Use your template to make four same-sized shoe pieces from the corrugated cardboard. Each snowshoe will be made by stacking two of your shoe pieces on top of each other.

LEFT SHOE

piece 1

piece 2

RIGHT SHOE

piece 3

piece 4

TIP
You could make only one shoe piece per foot, but your shoes won't be as strong!

Use a craft knife and cutting mat to cut out a slit on each side of the cardboard around your shoe. Place that piece on top of another shoe shape and mark the slits. Now cut out those slits. Glue the two shoe shapes together.

The slit should be as wide as a piece of duct tape.

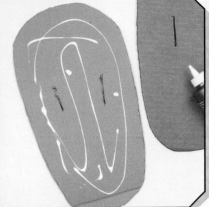

 Cut out small pieces of duct tape and wrap them around both pieces. Cut out designs from duct tape and decorate the shoe base.

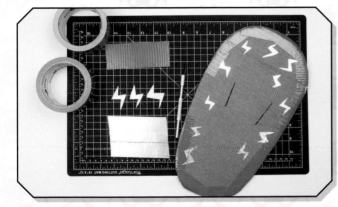

5 (To make top strap)

Cut out two similar-sized duct tape pieces to span over your foot.

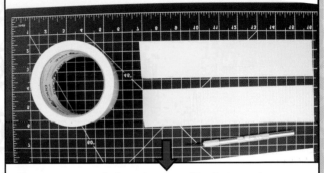

Flip one piece of clear tape so it's sticky-side up. Use a piece of tape to hold it down. Then place the other piece of tape on top.

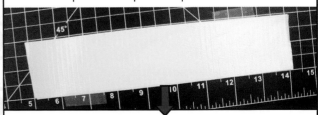

Tape it to the bottom of your shoe.

6 (To make back strap)

Cut out a piece of duct tape that will go around the back of your foot. Fold the duct tape in half to make a thin strap. Tape it to your top strap.

MAKERSPACE TIPS

Download tips and tricks for using this book and others in a library makerspace. Visit *www.capstonepub.com/dabblelabresources*

READ MORE

Sjonger, Rebecca. *Maker Projects for Kids Who Love Paper Engineering.* Be a Maker. New York: Crabtree Publishing Company, 2016.

Song, Sok. *Everyday Origami: A Foldable Fashion Guide.* Fashion Origami. North Mankato, Minn.: Capstone Press, 2016.

Ventura, Marne. *Awesome Paper Projects You Can Create.* Imagine It, Build It. North Mankato, Minn.: Capstone Press, 2016.

INTERNET SITES

FactHound offers a safe, fun way to find Internet sites related to this book. All of the sites on FactHound have been researched by our staff.

Here's all you do:
Visit *www.facthound.com*
Type in this code: 9781515793137

Super-cool stuff!

Check out projects, games and lots more at
www.capstonekids.com

ABOUT THE AUTHOR

LESLIE MANLAPIG

Leslie is a full-time mom and sometimes puppeteer who adores books, donuts, and the color yellow. She's always on the lookout for new ways to play and make things with kids. You can read about her family's creative and crafty adventures on her blog www.PinkStripeySocks.com.

Dabble Lab Books are published by Capstone Press.
1710 Roe Crest Drive
North Mankato, Minnesota 56003
www.mycapstone.com

Cataloging-in-Publication Data is available
on the Library of Congress website.
ISBN 978-1-5157-9313-7 (library binding)
ISBN 978-1-5157-9316-8 (eBook PDF)

Editorial Credits
Anna Butzer and Shelly Lyons, editors;
Aruna Rangarajan, designer;
Tracy Cummins, media researcher;
Tori Abraham, production specialist

Image credits: All photos by Leslie Manlapig and Enrico
Manlapig, except the following: Shutterstock: abeadev,
Design Element, Africa Studio, 3 (hand, phone), Boyan
Dimitrov, 13 (tape strips), Coprid, 13 (yarn), DSBfoto, 13
(velcro), Jakub Krechowicz, Design Element, KannaA,
Design Element, Kiselev Andrey Valerevich, Design Element,
kostudio, Cover, 10 (boy), KsanaGraphica, Design Element,
Picsfive, Design Element, Sylwia Brataniec, 13 (rope), Winai
Tepsuttinun, Back Cover (box), Design Element

Printed and bound in the United States of America.
010750S18